No More Bread!

by Alan Horsfield

illustrated by Jan D'Silva

Harcourt Achieve

Rigby • Saxon • Steck-Vaughn

www.HarcourtAchieve.com
1.800.531.5015

Characters

Me

Connie

Loren

2

Contents

Chapter 1

Boring!

We always have white bread. White bread for toast, white bread for sandwiches, white bread with jam. Always white bread.

I said, "We always have white bread, Mom."

"Yes," said my big sister, Connie, "it's always plain, old white bread!"

My little sister, Loren, said, "White bread for breakfast, white bread for lunch, and white bread for dinner!"

I had one of my sudden brainwaves.
"Mom," I said, "why don't you get a
bread maker?"

Mom looked at me without saying anything.
For a moment she almost smiled.

Mom looked at Connie. I could see Mom was keen. Her eyes lit up. She looked at Loren, thinking, her head to one side.

We all waited. Then Mom smiled her biggest smile ever. We all laughed!

Chapter 2

Mom the Baker

The very next day, Mom bought a new bread maker. It came with a shiny book called *How to Make Fantastic Bread.*

The bread maker was square and white. It had a little light. It had a buzzer to tell you when the bread was baked.

Mom spent all day reading her wonderful new bread book. She stared at her new bread maker.

The next day, Mom made bread. It was not white bread. It was . . . brown bread!

9

We could smell the fresh bread as we walked in the door. Kevin, who lives next door, could smell it, too. He ran into our kitchen sniffing the air like a hunting dog.

Mom said, "Hi Kevin. Would you like to try my fresh brown bread?"

Kevin licked his lips and nodded his head so fast I thought it might fall off. We all had hot, crusty brown bread for an afternoon snack.

Kevin said, "This is the best!"

We all agreed. Mom gave Kevin a big hunk
of brown bread to take home. He was really
pleased!

That night we had fresh brown bread with dinner. Dad liked it, too!

Mom said, "I'm a baker! I will make more bread."

For the next week, we had brown bread every day.

Chapter 3

No More Brown Bread

We always have brown bread. Brown bread for toast, brown bread for sandwiches, brown bread with jam. Always brown bread.

I said, "We always have brown bread, Mom."

"Yes," said Connie, "It's always brown bread!"

Loren said, "Brown bread for breakfast, brown bread for lunch, and brown bread for dinner!"

Mom looked at us and smiled. She took her book out and said, "No more brown bread then. I will make a surprise."

The next day, we had hot ginger bread. It was delicious. The next day, we had yellow banana bread. It was nice. Kevin came in to taste our bread nearly every day.

Next Mom made pumpkin bread. It was
bright orange. Then we had ham and onion
bread.

When I opened my lunch box at school, kids started giving me funny looks.

Raisin and nut bread came next. Then honey bread. Black Russian bread . . . Mom really loved her bread maker.

Apple bread, carrot bread, corn bread, tomato bread — everything but white bread. One day we were sitting at the table when Mom came in with her latest loaf of hot bread.

Mom put it on the table and cut it. It was
pink inside! I looked at the pink bread and
guessed, "Cherry bread?"

Connie said, "Raspberry bread?"

Loren whispered, "Strawberry?"

"Watermelon!" said Mom with a big,
big smile.

When the kids at school saw our pink
sandwiches, they all laughed. Kevin didn't say
anything. He just slowly shook his head.

"Would you like a sandwich?" I asked.

"They're pink!" he said with disgust.

Kevin stopped coming over to our place to
taste Mom's bread.

Chapter 4

It's Green

The next day, Mom placed her just-baked bread onto the table. We all shook our heads as she cut the bread. It was . . . green!

"Guess what?" she said.

"Beans?" I guessed.

"Peas?" said Connie.

"Lettuce?" whispered Loren.

"No, no, no," laughed Mom. "It's cabbage bread!"

We all pulled faces and said, "Yuck!"

The kids at school laughed and laughed at our green sandwiches.

Kevin said, "Have you tried purple bread?"

The kids all laughed again. I just glared at Kevin. I thought he was my friend!

We never have white bread. No white bread
toast, no white bread sandwiches, no white
bread and jam. Always funny bread.

I said, "We want white bread, Mom."

"Yes," said Connie. "Plain, old white bread,
please!"

Loren said, "White bread for breakfast,
white bread for lunch, and white bread
for dinner."

"Oh," said Mom. "Oh dear, oh dear. I do enjoy making things."

I wondered what else Mom could make. Then I had another great brainwave.

I said, "Why not get a juice maker? I love fresh juice."

"Orange juice," said Connie.

"Apple juice," said Loren.

"Even watermelon juice," I said.

Mom smiled and said, "What a good idea!"
So Mom got a brand new juicer with a shiny
book called *How to Make Fantastic Juice.*

Mom looked up from her wonderful new juice book and smiled. "Now I can make carrot juice, celery juice, prune juice, spinach juice, and even cabbage juice!"

My stomach did flip-flops.

Loren asked, "Mom, can we get an ice cream maker, too?"

Connie and I looked at Loren. We both shook our heads. I didn't even want to think about cabbage ice cream!

Glossary

brainwave
sudden clever idea

bread maker
a machine which mixes and bakes bread

crust
the hard, outside layer of bread

fantastic
very good or wonderful

hunting dog
a dog that searches for birds or animals

juicer
machine which gets liquid from fruit or vegetables

keen
eager, interested

strange
odd, unusual

Alan Horsfield

Alan enjoys nonsense rhymes and tongue twisters. Here are some of his favorites.

The boy stood on the burning deck,
His feet were full of blisters.
The flames came up and burned his pants,
And now he wears his sister's.

Try saying these tongue twisters aloud.
What noise annoys an oyster most?
A noisy noise annoys an oyster most.

Can you say this three times quickly?
A proper cup of coffee from a proper coffee pot.

Alan can get this right (sometimes)!
How much wood can a woodcutter cut,
If a woodcutter could cut wood?
He'd cut as much wood as a woodcutter would cut
If a woodcutter could cut wood.

Jan D'Silva

32